Contents

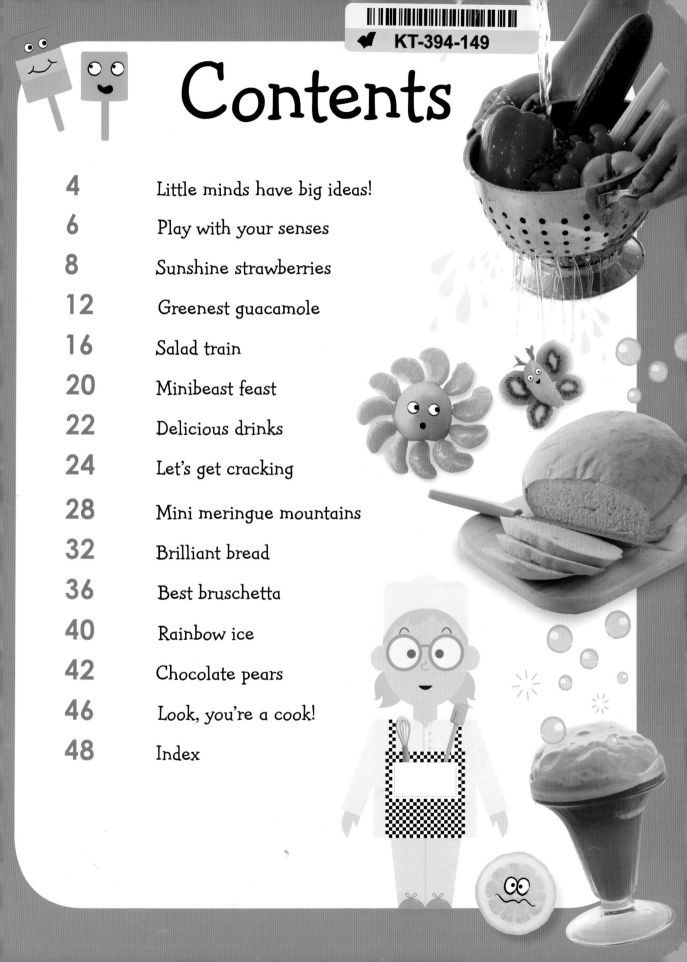

Little minds have big ideas!

You don't need a **tall white hat** or a **fancy restaurant** to be a great cook. You already have everything you need: **your brain** and **your amazing senses**!

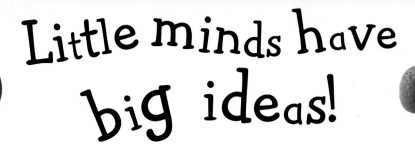

Curious questions

Cooking is so much more fun when you experiment. Here are some questions to ask yourself as you cook.

- How does my food look, feel, smell, sound, and taste?

- What changes do you notice in the food when you follow the recipes?

- Why do you think the ingredients change as you cook?

- How can I make food taste better?

LOOK

I'm a Cook

DK

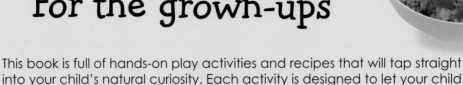
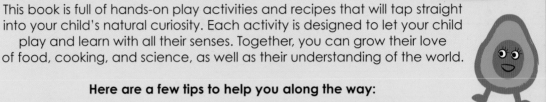

For the grown-ups

This book is full of hands-on play activities and recipes that will tap straight into your child's natural curiosity. Each activity is designed to let your child play and learn with all their senses. Together, you can grow their love of food, cooking, and science, as well as their understanding of the world.

Here are a few tips to help you along the way:

Your child should be supervised at all times when cooking and experimenting, but try to give them time and space to lead the direction of play. The questions in this book are suggestions. Let your child ask, and answer, their own questions.

•

Involve your child in each step of the recipes. Let them measure, mix, and follow the instructions. Encourage your child to taste as they cook, and allow them to modify the recipe if they would like to.

•

Adult Alert stars show where your child will need extra grown-up help. Before you start cooking, consider any kitchen hazards together and ways to avoid them. If your child has long hair, make sure it is tied back and out of the way.

•

Protect the area where your child will be playing, and encourage them to wear old clothes or an apron. Being prepared lets your child enjoy themselves to their fullest. Making a mess is part of fun and learning!

Adult ALERT!

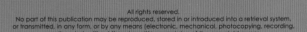

DK | Penguin Random House

Editor Hélène Hilton
Design and Illustration Rachael Parfitt Hunt
Additional Design and Illustration Charlotte Milner
Educational Consultant Penny Coltman
Photographer Dave King
Food Stylist Denise Smart
Jacket Designer Charlotte Milner
Jacket Co-ordinator Francesca Young
Editorial Assistance James Mitchem, Marta Rybarczyk
Design Assistance Eleanor Bates, Charlotte Bull, Rachael Hare, Pauline Korp
Pre-production Dragana Puvacic
Production Amy Knight
Managing Editor Penny Smith
Managing Art Editors Mabel Chan, Gemma Glover
Publisher Mary Ling
Creative Director Jane Bull

First published in Great Britain in 2017 by
Dorling Kindersley Limited
80 Strand, London WC2R 0RL

A CIP catalogue record for this book
is available from the British Library.
ISBN: 978-0-2412-8778-1

Printed in China

The publisher would like to thank the following for their kind permission to reproduce their photographs:
(Key: a-above; b-below/bottom; c-centre; f-far; l-left; r-right; t-top)

21 Getty: Photographer's Choice RF/Jon Boyes (cr). **25 Fotolia:** Eric Isselee (cr).
All other images © Dorling Kindersley

For further information see: www.dkimages.com

And a big thank you to all the little chefs who acted as models: Clara Fox,
Thomas Hellyar, Eddie Hunt, Elijah Knight, and Liyah Ventour-Russel.

A WORLD OF IDEAS:
SEE ALL THERE IS TO KNOW

www.dk.com

Your cooking senses

Brain

Your brain is not one of your senses, but it gathers information from them all and tries to understand it.

Hearing

Cooking causes lots of interesting sounds. What can you hear?

Sight

Food should look yummy as well as taste good!

Smell

Lots of the flavour of food comes from its smell. What clues can your nose give you?

Taste

Your tongue is your best chef's tool! Try your food as you cook it. Does it taste as good as it looks?

Touch

Your skin tells you how things feel. Be careful with objects that might be hot, cold, sharp, or that might hurt.

Let's see what we can do!

5

Play with your senses

When you eat, **all your senses** work as a **team** to tell your **brain** about what you're eating. Try these **kitchen experiments** to find out how **important** each of your senses really is.

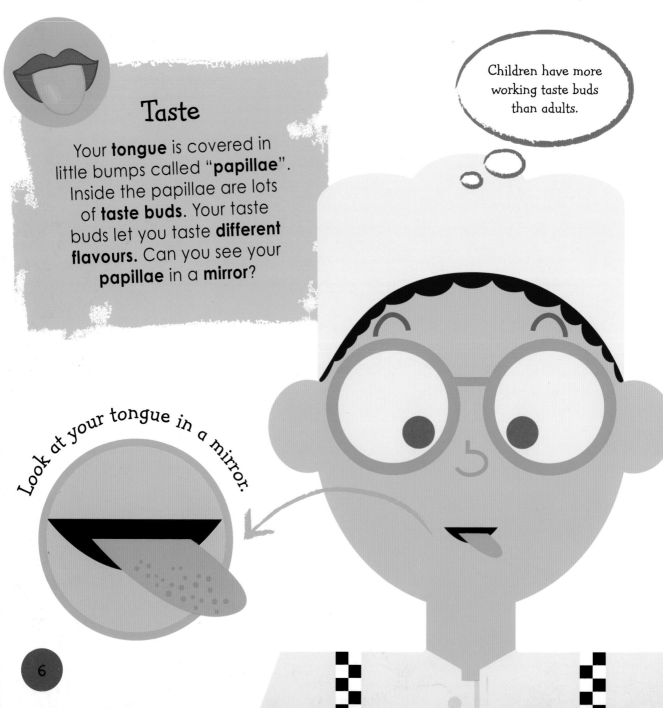

Taste

Your **tongue** is covered in little bumps called "**papillae**". Inside the papillae are lots of **taste buds**. Your taste buds let you taste **different flavours**. Can you see your **papillae** in a **mirror**?

Children have more working taste buds than adults.

Look at your tongue in a mirror.

Sight

Your **eyes** give you clues about food before you eat it. Wear a **blindfold** and **try** different foods. Can you **guess** what you're eating **without seeing it**?

Smell

Your sense of **smell** is even more sensitive than your sense of taste. Try **smelling** an **onion** before taking a bite from an **apple**. Does it change the **taste**?

Touch

The inside of your mouth can **feel** the different **textures** of food. Eat a **soft** slice of bread and a slice of **crunchy** toast. Which do you like **better**?

Hearing

Lots of food makes **sounds** as you **chew** it. Try eating **crunchy** food with your **hands over your ears**. Does this make a difference to the way the food **tastes**?

7

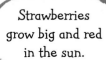

Strawberries grow big and red in the sun.

Sunshine strawberries

Lots of our **food**, such as **fruit** and **vegetables**, comes from **plants**. Can you guess where these **ingredients** have come from?

Makes 4 bowls

You will need:

300g (10oz) strawberries

4 tablespoons honey

Honey is made by bees. Bees work very hard to make honey from flower nectar.

You can grow strawberries in your garden or in a flower pot.

500g (1lb 2oz) yoghurt

a few mint leaves

gently wash

1

Wash the **mint** and **strawberries** with cold water.

Oops! I've lost my hat.

Strawberries are full of vitamin C, which helps your body fight germs.

Adult ALERT!

2

Remove the **stalks** and cut the **strawberries** in **half**.

9

3 Can you smell the mint?

mint

Tear the **mint** leaves into tiny teeny bits (as small as you can make them).

Yoghurt is a good source of calcium, which helps your body build strong bones and teeth.

4

Spoon the **yoghurt** into 4 bowls.

smooth and silky

Strawberries and mint are plants, but most yoghurt is made from cows' milk.

drizzle

SENSE-ible cooking

- Can you see the little seeds on the strawberries?
- Do you like the way the ingredients taste together?
- What does the smell of mint remind you of?
- Why do you think you need to wash the strawberries?

Yay! I made it!

Rabbits like mint as a treat!

5

Share out the **strawberries** and **mint** between the bowls and top with **honey**.

11

Greenest guacamole

Guacamole is made from **squashed-up avocados**!
It's a fresh, creamy, and **very tasty** recipe.

You will need:

2 medium
tomatoes

handful of coriander
(if you like it)

half an onion

3 ripe avocados

half a lime

salt and pepper
to season

Wash the tomatoes
and coriander before
using them.

1

Chop the **tomatoes** and **coriander** (if using) as small as you can. Carefully grate the **onion** with a cheese grater.

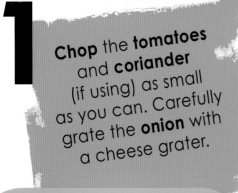

When you grate or cut onions, they release a gas that makes your eyes water.

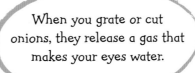

Adult ALERT!

chop chop scoop

2

Cut the **avocados** in half around the stone. Remove the stone and **scoop** the soft insides into a bowl.

Avocados are great at keeping your heart and brain healthy.

squash

Squashing the avocado gives it a slightly chunky texture.

3

Squash the **avocados** using a potato masher.

4

Add the chopped **ingredients** into the bowl and mix everything together.

Mix it all up!

5

Finish your guacamole by squeezing **lime juice** into it. **Season** with salt and pepper, then mix and serve.

SENSE-ible cooking

How does it feel to squash the avocado?

Does the avocado change colour?

Does the lime juice taste sour and acidic?

Sour science

Lime juice helps your guacamole stay **bright green**. Without lime juice, avocado turns **brown** when it touches the **air**. That's because the avocado **reacts** with a gas in the air called **oxygen**. Lime juice is full of **citric acid**, which **slows down** this reaction.

Citrus fruit all have citric acid in them. You can taste it – it's sour and might make you scrunch up your face! Which one of these citrus fruit tastes like it has the most citric acid?

orange

grapefruit

lemon

lime

blood orange

Salad train

Vegetables come in all **shapes**, **sizes**, **colours**, **textures**, and **tastes.** Make them even more **exciting** with this recipe. All aboooard! **Choo! Choo!**

You will need:

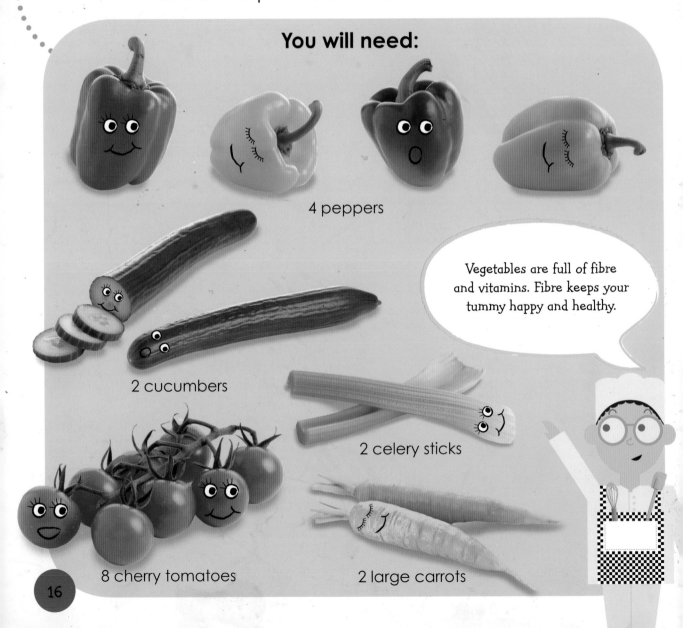

4 peppers

2 cucumbers

Vegetables are full of fibre and vitamins. Fibre keeps your tummy happy and healthy.

2 celery sticks

8 cherry tomatoes

2 large carrots

1

Wash the vegetables with cold water.

splash

2

Carefully **peel** the carrots. Then cut the celery, 1 cucumber, and 1 carrot into chunky sticks.

Be careful!

Adult ALERT!

17

Serve with your guacamole dip.

Time to make your **train**

guacamole

3

Adult ALERT!

To make the **carriages**, slice a side off the peppers and **scoop** out the seeds with a spoon.

Yay!

Fruit and vegetables both come from plants.

4

Fill the pepper carriages with the vegetable sticks and cherry tomatoes.

SENSE-ible cooking

Which vegetables have bumpy skin and which ones feel smooth?

Can you hear the vegetables crunch as you bite them?

Do all the vegetables taste the same? Which is your favourite?

Use carrot slices for wheels.

Make the front from cucumber and add celery leaves to look like steam.

All aboard!

Can you remember the names of all your ingredients?

Minibeast feast

Some **plants** hide their **seeds** inside **colourful fruit**. Fruit tastes **yummy** so animals eat it and **spread** the seeds. Fruit is also great for making amazing **minibeasts!**

You will need:

Try using herbs, icing, and chocolate chips to add faces and details to your minibeasts.

1 apple

1 apricot

a handful of grapes

1 tangerine or orange

1 kiwi

half a banana

Remember to wash your fruit.

Red ladybird

To make the body, cut a **red apple** in half and remove the core. Add a **grape** for the head and use **icing** to stick on **chocolate chips** for spots.

Summer sun

Peel a **tangerine** and arrange the segments around half an **apricot** to make a sun.

Busy butterfly

Peel and slice a **kiwi** for wings. Use an **orange** or large **tangerine** segment for the body, and use **mint** for antennae.

Snazzy snail

Draw an icing swirl on an apple slice to make a snail shell. Use half a **banana** to make the body and add **mint** antennae.

Cute caterpillar

Carefully push **grapes** onto a wooden skewer to make the body. Add **rosemary** leaves for antennae.

21

Delicious drinks

Drinks are **liquids,** which means that they **flow** and **change shape** to fit the glass they are in. Which of these **yummy liquids** is your favourite?

Fizzy float

Add 1 scoop of your favourite **sorbet** (we used raspberry) to a glass of **lemonade**. **Watch it fizz!**

Lemonade is full of carbon dioxide bubbles. Adding cold sorbet pushes all the bubbles out of the lemonade at once.

Monster smoothie

To make a monstrously **green** smoothie, you will need **2 kiwis**, **1 apple**, **half a cucumber**, and **a handful of spinach**. Put all your ingredients into a blender and **blend**!

Grenadine sinks to the bottom of the glass because it's heavier than orange juice. Scientists call this "density".

Blending fruit and veg cuts them up into tiny bits. The water inside comes out and the solid ingredients turn into a thick, flowy liquid.

Adult ALERT!

Sunset juice

Pour **orange juice** into a glass until it's **nearly full**. **Top up** with **grenadine syrup** to make a tropical **sunset**.

Let's get cracking

Eggs come from **animals**, but most of the eggs that we eat are **chicken eggs**. There are lots of ways to **cook** eggs. How do you like yours?

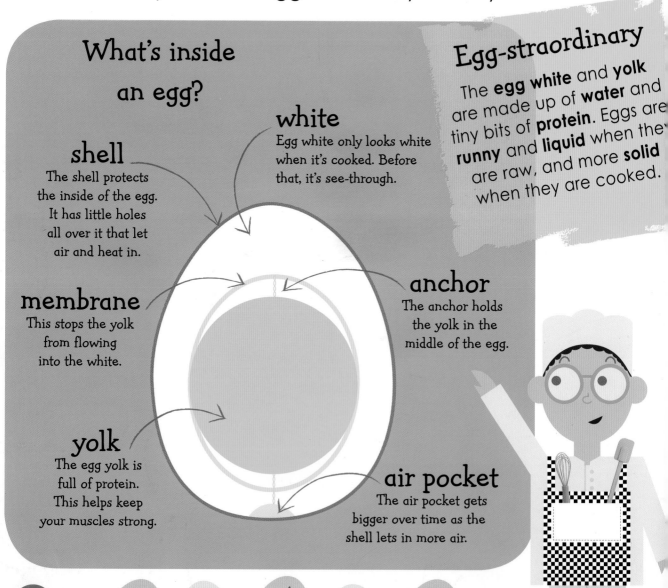

What's inside an egg?

white
Egg white only looks white when it's cooked. Before that, it's see-through.

shell
The shell protects the inside of the egg. It has little holes all over it that let air and heat in.

membrane
This stops the yolk from flowing into the white.

yolk
The egg yolk is full of protein. This helps keep your muscles strong.

anchor
The anchor holds the yolk in the middle of the egg.

air pocket
The air pocket gets bigger over time as the shell lets in more air.

Egg-straordinary

The **egg white** and **yolk** are made up of **water** and tiny bits of **protein**. Eggs are **runny** and **liquid** when they are raw, and more **solid** when they are cooked.

Egg-speriment

As eggs get **older**, the **air pocket** inside gets **bigger**. This makes the egg **float**. **Test** how fresh an egg is by dropping it in water. If it **sinks**, the egg is fresh. If it **floats**, the egg is a little older.

Can you see the tiny holes that let air through the shell?

Only girl chickens lay eggs. Girl chickens are called "hens". Do you know what boy chickens and baby chickens are called?

Animal egg mix-up

It's not just chickens that lay eggs!
Follow the trails to match the egg to the parent.

salmon

quail

duck

emu

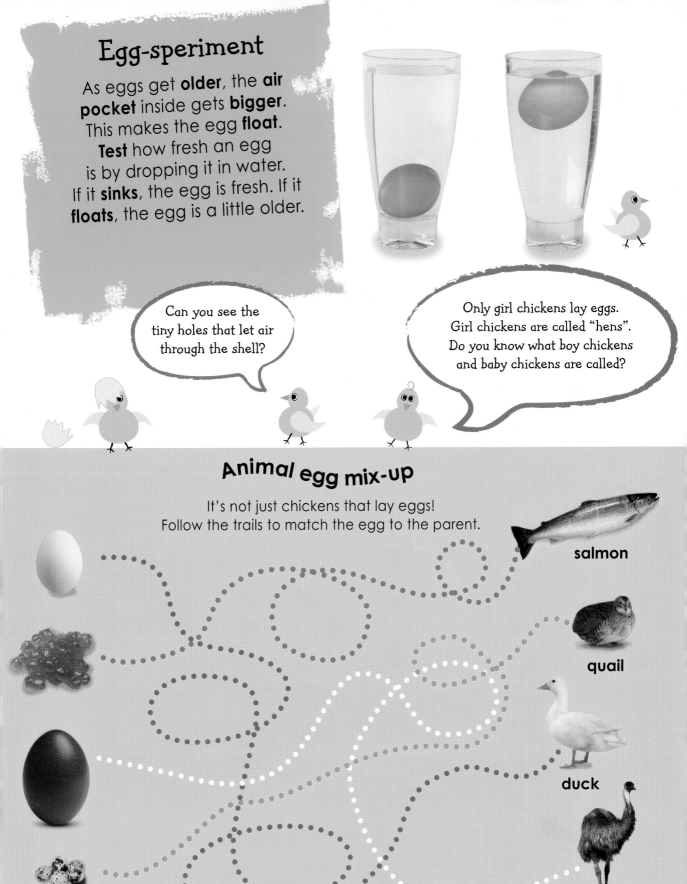

Happy eggs

Do you like your boiled eggs with a runny yolk or a hard yolk?

Boiled eggs

Gently lower eggs into a pan of **boiling water** using a big spoon. Cook them for **5 minutes** for **soft-boiled eggs**, or **8 minutes** for **hard-boiled eggs**.

A soft-boiled egg will have a runny yolk.

Adult ALERT!

A hard-boiled egg will have a solid yolk.

Chop the top off your eggs with a spoon, and enjoy.

soft-boiled egg

hard-boiled egg

26

runny egg

Adult
ALERT!

Fried egg

Carefully crack an egg into an oiled frying **pan**. Cook it over a **low heat**. Your egg is ready when the white has **completely set** and the yolk is **warm**.

Raw egg white is liquid so it spreads to take the shape of the pan. What happens when the white is cooked?

Cooking science

When you **cook** eggs, the bits of **protein** inside the white and yolk stop floating around. This makes the egg **solidify** (it stops being runny).

Mini meringue mountains

Eggs are great to make desserts **light** and **fluffy** because you can **whip lots of air into them**. These mini meringue mountains are crispy, sweet, and melt in your mouth.

Makes 12 meringues

You will need:

Sugar gives you lots of energy. But too much sugar can be bad for your body, so try not to have too many sweet treats.

2 eggs

100g (3½oz) caster sugar

1

To separate the **egg whites** from the **yolks**, carefully crack the eggs in half. Then tip the yolks **back and forth** between the half shells, letting the whites fall into a **bowl**.

egg white

Try not to drop any yolk in the bowl!

crack

2

Whisk the whites with an electric mixer until they make **stiff peaks**.

sugar

Adult ALERT!

3

Spoon in the sugar, **a little at a time**, and **whisk** until the mixture is completely **smooth**.

Ready!

When the mixture is stiff enough, you'll be able to hold the bowl upside down and nothing will fall out!

Make little meringue mountains.

4

Spoon the mixture onto a **baking sheet** to make meringue mountains.

Your meringues should stay as white as possible. If they start to look golden, turn the oven temperature down a little.

5

Bake in the oven at 120°C (250°F/Gas½) for **2 hours**, or until **crispy** all the way through.

Can you see the snowy mountains?

Meringue science

Whisking the egg whites creates foamy **air bubbles** inside. The **sugar** helps to **hold the foam** together, and the **heat** in the oven makes it **dry and crispy**.

SENSE-ible cooking

 Can you see the egg whites fluffing up as you whisk?

Can you hear the meringues crunching as you bite them?

Do the raw egg whites and the baked meringue feel very different?

Try your meringue with different fruit and toppings.

Brilliant bread

Bread is one of the **most popular foods in the world**. There are lots and lots of **different types** of bread, but this **easy-peasy recipe** is a yummy one to start you off.

You will need:

600g (1lb 5oz) strong white flour

yeast
1 tablespoon fast acting yeast

salt
1 teaspoon salt

Flour is made from a plant called wheat.

oil
2 tablespoons vegetable oil

400ml (14fl oz) warm water

Bread is one of the first types of food that humans ever made.

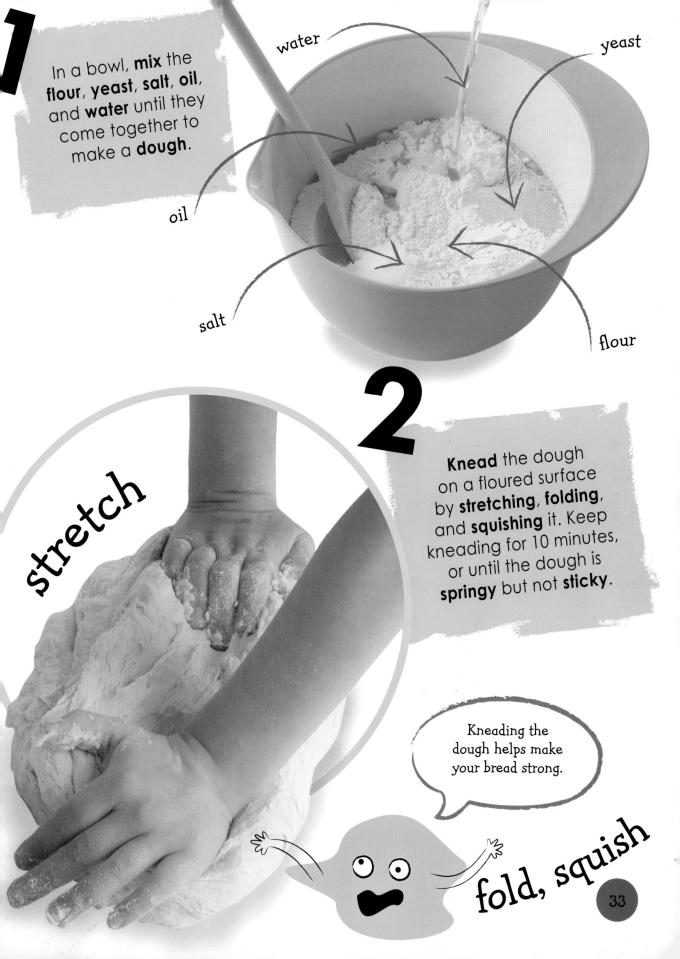

1

In a bowl, **mix** the **flour**, **yeast**, **salt**, **oil**, and **water** until they come together to make a **dough**.

water

yeast

oil

salt

flour

stretch

2

Knead the dough on a floured surface by **stretching**, **folding**, and **squishing** it. Keep kneading for 10 minutes, or until the dough is **springy** but not **sticky**.

Kneading the dough helps make your bread strong.

fold, squish

3

Place the dough on a baking tray and leave it in a **warm** place for 45 minutes, or until it has **doubled in size**. Preheat the oven to 220°C (425°F/Gas 7).

Adult ALERT!

Watch me get bigger and bigger!

Why does it grow?

Yeast is a very tiny fungus that eats the **sugar** inside the **flour**. When it does, **bubbles** of a gas called carbon dioxide are created and make the bread **rise**.

4

Gently **brush** the dough with warm **water**. This will help make the bread **crusty**.

34

5 Bake in the oven for 30 minutes, or until the bread is cooked **all the way through**. Let it cool down before slicing.

Tap the bottom of your bread. If it's cooked, the air bubbles inside will make it sound hollow.

tap

tap

Adult ALERT!

SENSE-ible cooking

Can you smell your bread baking in the oven?

Can you hear the hollow bubbles inside your bread when you tap it?

Does your bread taste different to bread you can buy in the shops?

Best bruschetta

This tasty **Italian** snack is a great way to enjoy your **brilliant bread.** Toast it and top it with **fresh ingredients** that all your **senses** will love.

Makes 4 slices

You will need:

6 tomatoes

Your brilliant bread

Tomatoes and garlic are both great at helping your body fight off germs.

4 tablespoons olive oil

1 garlic clove

Season with us!

salt and pepper to season

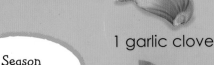

handful of basil leaves

1

Wash and chop your **tomatoes** and **basil**. Peel your **garlic** clove.

wash

chop   peel

2

Carefully cut **4 slices** from your loaf of **bread**.

Adult ALERT!

Ouch!

lightly toast

3

Lightly **toast** your bread slices in a **pan** or a **toaster**.

Adult ALERT!

4

Rub the **garlic** clove onto your toasted bread to **flavour** it.

Toasting the bread

Heating up the bread creates a **chemical reaction** that changes the **sugar** inside it. This reaction changes the bread's **colour**, **texture**, and even **taste**.

5

Top your garlic toast with the **chopped tomatoes** and **basil**.

Mmm!

Drizzle

with

olive oil.

Season with salt and pepper.

SENSE-ible cooking

Can you feel a difference between the bread and the toast?

How does the garlic smell?

Taste your bruschetta before and after seasoning. Which taste do you prefer?

Do you think you could turn toast back into bread?

Rainbow ice

When flowy **liquids** get **cold** enough, they **freeze** and turn into stiff **solids**. Try making these frozen **ice lollies** to enjoy on a hot sunny day.

I've been frozen upside-down!

Frozen yoghurt

Poke a plastic spoon through the lid of a **mini yogurt pot**. Leave in the **freezer** overnight then pop it out of the pot to eat.

fruit juices

yoghurt

lolly stick

The warmth from your tongue melts the ice lollies.

spoon

Layered ice lollies

Choose your favourite **fruit juices** and freeze them **one layer at a time** in a plastic cup. Once a layer is frozen, **pour** in the next one and **freeze again**. Don't forget a **lolly stick!**

40

See-through lollies

Put your favourite **fruit** in an ice lolly mould or plastic cup and pour in your **favourite clear drink** (we used lemonade). **Freeze overnight**.

lemonade

fruit

From water to ice

When liquids get cold enough, the tiny bits inside (molecules) hook onto each other and stop flowing around. The liquid freezes into a solid. Freezing is the opposite of melting.

liquid water

solid ice

Try using a thermometer to check the temperature in your home, outside, in the fridge, and in the freezer.

Temperature

We use "temperature" to **measure** how **hot** or **cold** things are. Water freezes into ice at **0°C** (32°F), but different liquids freeze and melt at different temperatures.

Chocolate pears

Impress your friends with this **super scientific**, and super **tasty**, **dessert**. It's a great recipe to **experiment** with different **temperatures** and **play** with **flavours**.

Serves 4

You will need:

4 pears (fresh or canned)

150g (5½oz) dark chocolate

4 scoops of vanilla ice cream

75g (2½oz) icing sugar

150ml (5fl oz) single cream

1

Carefully **peel** the **pears** and **cut** them in **half**. Remove the **cores** with a spoon.

scoop scoop

peeler

Adult ALERT!

Pears are a great healthy snack because they're full of fibre and vitamins.

2

Break the **chocolate** into **pieces** and place them into a small saucepan.

Snap!

Mmm!

Adult ALERT!

Pour

3

Add the **icing sugar** and **cream** to the pan and place it over a **very low heat**.

Dark chocolate has less sugar in it than milk chocolate, so it's a bit healthier.

43

4

Keep **stirring** as the chocolate **melts**, until the sauce is **smooth** and **runny**.

It's getting hot in here.

5

Share out the **pears** between **4 bowls**. Add a scoop of **vanilla ice cream** and top with your **chocolate sauce**.

If the sauce is too chocolatey for you, try stirring in a little more cream.

Adult ALERT!

44

Cacao beans

Chocolate is made from **cacao** beans, which are the **seeds** of the cacao tree. The cacao beans are ground up and mixed with sugar and milk to make chocolate.

Cacao beans only grow in hot places.

cacao beans

cacao pod

SENSE-ible cooking

What happens when the hot chocolate sauce touches the cold ice cream?

Does the sauce smell very chocolatey?

Taste some ice cream with and without the chocolate sauce. How is it different?

A melty experiment

When chocolate gets hot enough, it turns from a hard solid into a flowy liquid. You can experiment to find out how hot chocolate needs to be to melt. What happens when you put a piece of chocolate...

...in the fridge.

...in your hand.

Dark chocolate, milk chocolate, and white chocolate are made differently. They melt at different temperatures.

...on your tongue.

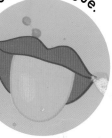

...outside in the sun.

...outside in the shade.

Look, you're a cook!

Chefs rely on their senses and skills to follow a set of **steps** when they cook. Think about your own cooking. Can you follow **the chef's steps?**

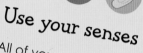

Use your senses

All of your **senses** work as a **team** to help you enjoy your food. Think about your **favourite** recipes. What **smells, textures, colours,** and **sounds** made them so **special?**

Make it yummy

Try to **taste** your ingredients **as you cook. Play** and **experiment** with recipes to make them your own. How can you make your food taste **even better?**

Stay safe

Chefs have to be **careful** in the kitchen. Always ask an **adult** to cook with you, and make sure to **wash your hands** with **scap** before you begin.

What's your favourite food? Why?

Be creative

Chefs love to **make up** new recipes. Start with your **favourite ingredients** and **create** your very own dish. What will you **name** it?

Well done!

....

(Write your name here.)

is a cook!

Index